INFINITE ARRIVALS

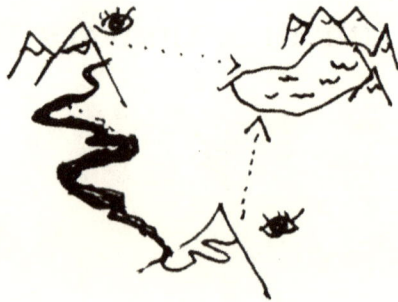

INFINITE ARRIVALS

NICK MAIONE

Angelico Press

First published in the USA
by Angelico Press 2023
Copyright © Nick Maione 2023

For information, address:
Angelico Press, Ltd.
169 Monitor St.
Brooklyn, NY 11222
www.angelicopress.com

ppr   978-1-62138-925-5
cloth   978-1-62138-926-2

Cover art by Nick Maione
Cover design by Lauren Peters-Collaer
Author photo by James Napoli
Book design by Michael Schrauzer

for my family

CONTENTS

BOOK II

If we could but find a rhythm of being which could balance a contemplative grace, a poetry of motion, and an accompanying stillness and silence, our pilgrimage though this world would flow in beauty through the most ragged and forsaken heartlands of confusion and dishevelment.

—John O'Donohue

From San Trophime Basilica
Arles, France—August 25

To The Tomb of Saint James
Santiago de Compostela, Spain—November 1

1,100 miles (1,770 km)

BOOK I

Tous les matins nous prenons le chemin
tous les matins nous allons plus loin.
Jour après jour la route nous appelle
c'est la voix de Compostelle.
Ultreïa! Ultreïa! Et suseia!
Deus adjuva nos.
        — Jean-Claude Benazet, Le chant des pèlerins
                                 de Compostelle

On a dark night
I must be a lucky one

    I got out unseen
    I got out unseen

On a dark night
I must be a lucky one

    I got out unseen
    from my silent house

On a dark night
I must be lucky

    I got out unseen
    I got out unseen

On a dark night
I must be in luck

    I got out unseen
    from my silent home

> Bearing love like anxious fire

I got out unseen
I got out

> Bearing love's anxious fire

I left my silent house
unseen

> Bearing love, an anxious fire

I got out unseen

> Bearing love's anxious fire

I got out unseen,
my silent home

song in the kitchen with the sisters making sauce
song for the sick horse with flies in his eyes
song of a yellow house the yellow of fresh butter
work song to repair our damaged ship
song in Euskara along canals sharing honey
song for Suzanne and the smell of wet paint
songs without plan

[AN ARRIVAL]

First steps this morning through yellow fields along the
Petit Rhône. But turned around: left phone in Van Gogh's
bedroom. Once back in Arles (all flower and brick, my
name still chalked on the door of the Vincent-themed
hostel) bells ring Sunday Mass at St. Trophime. Always we
begin again. I'm learning, and being treated with a bit of
gentleness, my body isn't refusing me its services, Vincent
told Theo from here. Let's backstitch this child's beginning
lest it come undone, St. Louis told St. James from there.
The pew cool, my backpack warm. The Narrow Way homily
is the priest saying *chemin* over and over. Mass ends in
procession for St. Cesaire, who swings us around the
ambulatory, past his relics, and towards the bright doorway
gaining terrible speed. We're flung at last out onto the hot
square as from a trebuchet, body parts all singing their
trajectory. Cathedral-to-cathedral as one case may be. *Bon
chemin!* a stranger calls out, another homilist. Something
great is always coming true. The music ends, people start
talking and stop walking. I, as it happens, do not————

FURTHERANCE

First your face.
The sun blesses it
off. Then night chars
your belly with the scent
of mountain mint.

At the next crossing
you look ahead
and say
this will make me too different
from the ones I love.

KIND OF LIGHT

I thank you for the wonder of my being
in this turquoise river, teens leaping
off Devil's Bridge trading dusts
with kestrels, breast pocket filled
with prayers and grapes, semi-sweet and taken
right off the vine with one hand by day,
your hand with my other by night
on a gym cot far from home, torch
that generates the ground it illumines,
cantaloupe jam that cherishes the mouth it touches,
the humiliating and swell fullness of everything
to come, a one-step-become, foes well-dressed
as sunflowers, watchers for the dawn,
all that we can ever long for as enough.

PROVENDER

The Murcian girl from earlier
is by herself at the supermarket
buying two beers
for her freckled throat.
The Balkan musician
whose fret hand by day
dammed and pooled us people
in the summer street
now counts out from that palm
one coin at a time
for crackers. I am offended
that they are strangers to me.
It will happen again in Sorèze
sitting in an empty church
listening to the organist
practice thinking she's alone.

MORE AND MORE

I acted like a blind dog in Montpellier
when I heard the Vespers violin —
the young useless dog I saw
that morning, chained to a stake
in the cracked ochre yard,
surprisingly healthy,
who stood up to wag or bark
in not-quite-someone's direction
when he heard the master,
or man, approach.

song in Portuguese dancing with Alexandra
song of french horns on the other sides of walls
song about what we brought a long way
song for what disappears in spite of
song to remind God this was his idea
husband song of Nathalie's cancer
lip-synched song by the saint's silver tomb

[AN ARRIVAL]

The grandmother using the open hatch of the butcher
van as a bench. The grandfather in the driver's seat
asleep from wine and sun. He wakes too hot, starts the
engine, seeking shade. Does not know about his wife in
the back. We scream, he's too hard of hearing, it's too
late. Her dragging heels spray grass into the air. Stockings
flash at a height and speed uncommon when attached
to a grandmother. Now motionless on the grass in the
hot farm silence. No, she's up on all fours. No, she's at
the window cursing her idiot husband in French. He
doesn't let it get to him; he's already asleep. She walks
back to the picnic blanket. Fills a glass of wine. Deep sigh.
Nicolas her grandson is the first to start laughing and
she is next and now everyone is dying. When the time
comes to part ways, her kiss misses my cheek hits my lips
and laughter. The human is a clumsy goodbyer———

DISTANCE LOVES BLUE

Keyhole of another beautiful
locked church in Languedoc
my lips brush lightly
as I look through, kneeling—

I see a woman dressed in blue
who plays a melodica for her son.
He dances above, a prince
twirled on a wooden balcony.
Her back is arched. So is his.
It is hard to believe in the difficult geometries

of what ends up happening.
She sends seven notes up to her boy.
He lowers down to her two red ropes.

GOOD SHOW, GOOD SHOW

I fall asleep feeling my heartbeat in sore feet.
I wake some hour in the dark and know
what time it is like this—
if the pulse is a distant, workable ache,
it will be almost morning; if it's still an alarm
of pain blaring up to the knees,
the night's not gotten far.
I lie awake feeling almost prized
to be a terrain that time struggles to cross.
To be a sundial that reads itself in the dark,
having found it best to look
not where the shadow points
but the quality of its edges—
how sharp or soft where the borders are,
how frayed where I've sewn it on.

TWO SONGS
FOR CARDABELLE

Acanthus fleur we nail to our door,
Remain outside while we pour champagne

Heart medallion, wounded home decor,
Be deathless and help us field our shame

Or, better:

Cardabelle!
Pretty thistle,
silent whistle,
for the rain

THE LAST WORDS THE MAGPIE HEARD
BETWEEN HIS FRIEND GIANT AND
HIS OPPONENT SAINT GUILHEM, WHO
BREACHED THEIR CLIFFTOP CHATEAU
BY DRESSING AS A MAIDEN CARRYING
WATER, HIDING JOYEUSE (HIS COUSIN
CHARLEMANGE'S MIRACULOUS SWORD)
IN HIS JUG, TO DO BATTLE ON BEHALF
OF THE VILLAGE BELOW

You choose how then, Saint

    Sunflowers

Is it allowed?

    For you as for them

Is it enough?

    It will have to be

    [The wounded Giant walks
    to the edge of his stone house,
    looks down the cliff
    at the yellow fields below
    and whispers to himself:]

What my death is embedded in —

    [Lets himself fall,
    the strands of his thin beard dancing
    on his scarred face
    a child's smile
    as it smashes into the clay

    Magpie flies off,
    Guilhem in tears]

ALONG THE WAY

In the dim woods
a mother and daughter

hunt mushrooms
wearing the same blue linen.

Count the steps I take
to pass them —

That many times
I am not dying

to tear off this
loneliness dress.

song of cold mornings, cold breakfast, warm coffee
song to the smell of nearby figs
troubadour song in Occitan
song to the hands of the man who taught us to peel chestnuts
song having a chestnut only dinner
song finding a dead bat
song for the priest who fainted in his soup

[AN ARRIVAL]

While I'm writing this in Marciac, Gilles bikes up to the
café, says after all Gabriel and Vicki want to sing songs in
the back garden. I follow him home. And it is as he says.
We drink homemade liquor. The guitar gets passed. My turn.
I sing I intended not to stop in this town. I sing I have
almost nothing to do with my being here. Vicki calls it a
true folk song. Now Gilles is getting loose, belting favorites
from his Cabo Verde days, incredible baritone. Light hits
the spire. Incredible thing about loss; it too gets lost. The
false bottom riddled with the same infinity it came from.
The blessèd sifts through. Or stays behind. Whichever is
better. For dessert we eat yogurt with chestnut purée ———

ONE WORD

Two slugs died kissing.
I found them.

Dried black smears
that didn't choose grass
before a noon sun.

I am far removed
from the quick evaporating
of worlds.

And that is close enough
for now. Oh, but
I love you.

OhbutIloveyou,
like it were one word

for now

that was impossible
to say,

I mean,
to ever not shout
at the earth.

FOR JOSEPH
(OF MY PAPER
ICON BOOKMARK)

The Lord will one day walk
with your posture on the beach.
He'll display your manual ease
when gutting a fish for his friends.
Will learn to send the voice through
a crowded workshop, or clean
across a field. He will know to keep
your genius way of keeping silent
when he knows he is being
cheated on a deal.
I see now, as you hold him,
how he looks at you looking at Mary,
who looks at the child
seeing you do that
through laminated goldlight.
Peace so free will cost us everything
I mumble, hoping you, at least, will
correct me.

CATCH

My back against a tree alone
like an affirming hum
one person extends alone
after the good laughter of a group.

A red kite hunts overhead.
The smell of familiar fields coats my throat.
The sun turning my skin the color
of near-dead sunflowers.

I unwrap the last of the wild boar
sausage got from a farmer several villages ago.
How joy and why now—
No reason. That's fine, that's fine.
I open the knife.
It has only taken, what, four hundred miles?
That's fine it's easy to slice into.

GIVING IT SHAPE

It tricks the soul into loving
for a while what she already is,

pens her bewildered movement in
with peregrine permission,

makes her sit down on the floor of her life
to find the big things favorably scaled.

It lets a day fit into one hand, like a rattle,
with its worries many beads stuck inside.

She hears for once the sound a day makes.
Practicing. That is the point.

On the stone bridge a crisp noise,
or lingering bellsong in a tower,

leaving friends at a wedding?
One way to teach a child anything

is to let her think she is playing,
and the game is ending soon.

song to the wetness in the rock
song to who made water so heavy
song eating pulpo in Melinde
song of the Visigoth ruins
song to the baker's children in order to buy bread
song buying eggs
song buying beer with lemonade
song because there is a difference between a bell and a picture of a bell

[AN ARRIVAL]

Tomorrow I will meet Pierre, a Swiss. I will be the other
obvious pilgrim eating alone. He will gesture for me to
join him. *I am here to walk and admire God alone but we must
not be silly about it,* he'll say when I sit down. Married
with two sons. Fell off a horse at sixteen. Crippled his
whole life until a recent surgery allowed him to walk
freely. I'll decide that's why he's out here, to uncoil the
life's-worth of walking wound inside him. I will never
see or speak to him again for the rest of my life. But first
Pierre will refuse not to treat me to lunch. While he pays
the bill he'll tell me *I was supposed to be in the World Trade
Center on Sept. 11 but missed two subway trains so I just stayed
uptown to try your American pancakes. They're very good*————

NO WORDS BUT
AWARENESSES OF RESCUINGS

If you see them Mother please tell them I'm a poor mourning
pilgrim bound for Canaan land.
—Sacred Harp 417

A toddler in a father's arms
thinking it's wise to pretend to be asleep
because if he knows I am awake
he will make me walk upstairs by myself

An adolescent asking are we there yet
in a voice farther and farther from my own
trying to last with no good answer
like a moving target all the theres along the way

An adult walking by myself thinking I'm wise
thinking about the desires on earth
how they are all desires to survive the wreckage
mouths intact enough to drink peace straight
    from a famous river

AN UNORGANIZED RESPONSE

I have traded an old bridge a song
    and drawn the beautiful spire.
I laughed in the rain
    and held silence up to constellations.
But now I try to floss my teeth in windows
    across from more basilicas.
Wait until the Pyrenees loom to apply cream
    where it is sure to burn cold.
To a dying bean field's orange invitation to live
    up to my own life
    I drain blisters, depending on the hue.
And on the flight home I'll pass gas over lakes
    of Newfoundland sunlight.
Who will tell me how to pair magnitudes?

SONG

I should have a song
    by now
for seeing you leave
    my life
like a hare leaves
    a dirt trail
I walk
    for sunflowers.

It could begin
    ding,
   dong,
    ding —
tomorrow is a bell is
   a town I'm going to.

DRAW A LINE CONNECTING EACH OF
THESE THREE SPIRITUAL VALUES OF
WABI-SABI TO THEIR CORRESPONDING
COMPLIMENT IN THE HAZELNUT-
BASED REVELATIONS OF JULIAN OF
NORWICH. IT MAY HELP TO HOLD AN
ACTUAL HAZELNUT, OR CHESTNUT, AS
THE CASE MAY BE:

· Incomplete   · God keeps it

· Impermanent   · God loves it

· Imperfect   · God made it

song for impossible gallantry in a land smelling of garlic
song washing underwear in the sink
song to the calf-massage machine
waltz for Patricia and Piedad in the dining room
song of the intentionally misaligned arch
song of things saints hold in statues
song of thirty miles in the rain and the rain and the rain therein
song anyway we don't remember the words to

[AN ARRIVAL]

A lot begins in kitchens in this life; it's worth saying.
Our host gives seltzer and seats us around the table.
I can't understand his French but his warm, worn
voice breaks my heart. There is something happening.
Later on someone hands me a book titled *Dachau, Mon
Baptême!* Dachau, My Baptism. Written by our host.
Nineteen-year-old Jewish medical student deported
in 1944. Eighty-nine year-old doctor running a pilgrim
shelter / crisis pregnancy call center out of his home.
He will die next year. Tonight I sleep in his daughter
Carine's old bedroom, surrounded by her childhood
paintings. In the morning we sing a hymn around his
office desk, crying, not understanding why. He kisses us
one at a time as we walk out the door into the southern
sun of Castres. My nakedness illumined for so many
miles. Squinting now (right now) from that light———

for Dr. Bernard Py
(1925–2014)

DU PAIN

Morning
    always breaks

open lies the night

speaks.

ONCE

It was enough that a real person lived
and thought something was worth mentioning.
Like today someone found himself putting his hands
in a shallow river imagining a wife he doesn't have.
He splashes the cold water over his head and neck.
It drips off his throat, the tip of his nose, his parted lips.
When it touches his hands again it is so warm.

I END THE POEM EATING FIGS

I'm hungry.

Ripe figs give up their shape under my boot.

When I look down and notice
they stain the clay deeply,

I walk my face into a thorn branch.

∽

Let the sun come to dry the dark moisture
around the mouth of the man
who failed the song he loves

—*and for all we know all songs to come,*
says the hand in a frayed sock,

with a lost child's face drawn on it

that speaks sometimes when the meaning doesn't arrive
and I've paid difficult attention.

It's not a good mask.

∽

God's no monkey's paw papa
though sometimes he is terrible

and gives what we ask for,
says Doctor Teresa.

∽

It all may well be true. But what I hear today is—

The Heart is Good

Look Up, See Figs

Are They Stones? No

HOME

In her dirt slippers she
padded through the kitchen door.
It isn't clear how long they have lived
in this farmhouse without the mother.
The father invited me in for water.

He is old to have so young a daughter.
When he speaks kindness carves his face
so they are young in unison and marooned
on their orchard together.

Their home is a magnificent mess. I get stuck to things.
Everything is coated with a cider
just-pressed from the perfect whirrings of a lonely child
and the bruised fruit of her woemason father,
trying to raise his memories
as well as his daughter.

With two small hands she brings me
a glass of water. I point to my chest —
Nicolas. She looks at her father
and speaks a name I cannot follow.

Dulcement, he nods. Slowly,
I sink into the solemnity of a daughter,
an oak trunk soaked in a difficult brown river
until its later carving by another.

She speaks her name again — *Solene* —
and runs out back to the garden, divining
the direction I have to go.

song at altitude with the dizzy swallows
song down low with lizards in the valley
song for giving a drawing to Sister Christine
song with the wheelchair riders for the strangeness in our bodies
song in the dark across candles
song as creased as a map
song on day 40

39

[AN ARRIVAL]

Nine at night, after eleven hours of pavement, getting lost,
and the rain. I stand in front of the door of the dark and
empty shelter, too late to get a key. A problem, yes. But
can't I go back to the village, ask around for a bed? Yes.
Cough up extra for the chambre d'hôte by the pizzeria? Yes.
Roll out the sleeping pad? Yes. A problem's not a problem,
it's just the next thing you're doing—what a day mostly is.
The good thing is harder to take. To know what to do with.
We're amateurs in abounding but seasoned warriors of want.
I stare at the door handle like it's the outstretched hand of
someone who ought to slap me. I reach out mine———

A POLLARD WILLOW TREE
CALLS TO VAN GOGH

Vincent I am a clenched fist
In a stranger's field I stand
For nothing a mangle of knobs
Wrecked eyes in a face with nothing to show or say

I'm twisted and strange with feeling
I show and say too much stunned wondering
After the farmer carted my flesh away
If it is like you say Vincent—
There is no useful difference
Between happiness and unhappiness
As people are sad and fine like fires
Inside their own houses smoke rising
From their chimneys nostalgia offered up I see

This low sun is someone else's halo
Out here our whoness is darkened
We are not sowers fathers friends
Or lovers but I speak for myself
How long Vincent how long?
Bring your reed pen tipped with woeful courage
This is worse than I feared—
I have been loved

If nothing else come draw it
Consider me with that ink
That makes come true and plainly
What it seeks urgently to know hurry
Someone has seen us
She is tripping over hills shouting wait with garlands
Hurry it won't be long she is running to ruin
Our unhappiness with her hands
And we will have to let her won't we

NOTHING COMES

But what is human
we approach
within licking distance
of the Pyrenees

This holy tastes
like pretty horses on fire
      speeding across a field

Here comes Bernadette
Today she is a young man
with a shotgun and an orange vest

I ask in a cobbled, trailmade French,
What are you hunting?

Sanglier, she says
smiles through two hooked fingers
on either side of his mouth

My throat acts allergic
to all the things we could do
if we believed we were loved

The sun is hot and loud
and the shadows are complete
where they are complete

Bon courage! as we part
like two humans trying
to stay on the walking side
of the water

TORCHLIGHT PROCESSION

Immaculate Mary, our hearts are on fire.
—Lourdes Hymn

Isaac of Stella says
the Lord chose to heal the leper by touching him
though a word would have sufficed

We should heal
not in the easiest
but in the most loving
way possible

And there is no touch
there is no way
there is no health
there is no warmth
        no friend
        no fire
        no heaven
        no joy
there is no thing like it,
        the hell of Mercy

where children get broiled
by the utterly attendant

by what will be hours

and fall off the bone
and into ourselves-as-God's
and some keep going
and some don't
Mother

It's Wednesday

43

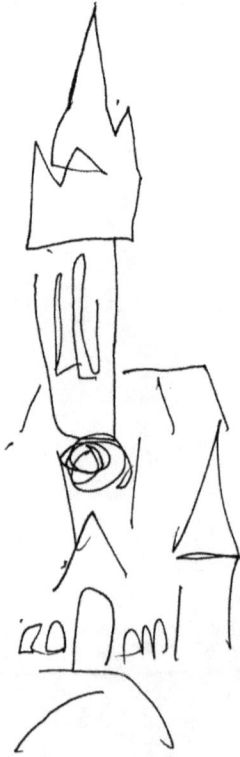

BOOK II

El camino se compone de llegadas infinitas.
                                —Atahualpa Yupanqui

Love made a sphere
And we scratched its surface

    And its surface scratched us
    It scratched us

Love made a sphere
And we scratched its surface

    And its surface scratched us
    But not our surface

Love made a sphere
And we scratched its surface

    And it scratched us
    It scratched us

Love made a sphere,
We did scratch its surface

    And its surface scratched us
    but not our surface

Grey and Gold and Black and Green came out

It scratched us
Its surface scratched us

Grey and Gold and Black and Green came out

It scratched us
But not our surface

Grey and Gold and Plum flowed

And it scratched us
Its surface scratched us

Grey-Gold and Black and

Its surface scratched us
But not our surface

song eating a cool peach stunned this should be
song of the spine under Slavic chiropractor hands
song for Alfonso trying to touch your fontanelle
song because of architecture
song for chain smoking clergy
song of home nobody required of us
stringed song for Oliver

[AN ARRIVAL]

I was finished. After all God does not ask us to be
successful, but faithful. Not to accomplish some task but
to be someone. With whole constellations of reasons in my
sky, I was finished. Then that evening a message arrived
from my childhood friend: *meeting you in Spain!* —... My
reasons now dim stars; gone when gazed at directly. I
was not finished. In fact, tried the Roman marching
technique a horse farmer demonstrated: *like this you make
eighty kilomètre just one day.* Essentially, jog as often as walk,
alternate every ten minutes. He was also ex-military and
an alpine guide; I lasted one hour. Still made it a day
early to surprise Zac, who'd tried to surprise me as well.
St. James got us both, putting us a few feet from each
other on a crowded Pamplona street. I hear my name. An
astonishment of the familiar in a far country. What the
heart is — something great always coming true. Friend
laughing in a blue hiking shirt in time. Before drinks, a
practical provision: we combine laundry back at the refugio.
While out celebrating our providential good fortune, our
clothes are stolen out of the dryer. Everything new———

WE TRY WRITING
A PILGRIM PRAYER

Lord you know my inmost chafing
    You've fitted me for these boots in my mother's womb
You are a balm to my most secret hotspots
    Better is the light of faith than a 1000 lumen headlamp
When I am weary and cannot achieve
    Your saints perform great miracles for me
Easily hitting 3-pointers from half court
    Whilst sitting in lawn-chairs—...

PYRENEAN GOODBYE

When finally on the mountain
you don't see the mountain.
Its gorgeous profile just isn't visible
the way it had been, sorry,
but look how fine and far it puts the horizon.

Soil on lips from the kissing-game,
still too close for words —
Words used backwards is *sword,*
and *towards* is also gone a while.

In one direction, toeprints
of the beautiful shepherdess.

In another, weather systems
in ambush of kingdoms.

IN THE MEANTIME

We stop to wrap Zac's foot,
share a chocolate bar and a pear using a knife
I got him yesterday for his birthday.
Snacking towards Bethlehem, he says.
I try to be encouraging, *don't worry your feet*
will thicken not just more callouses
that's already happening but thicken as feet
grow flesh become more foot there.
Pull off my boot as proof.
Entirely impossible to notice.
He still doesn't believe he saved me.

EVERYTHING NEW

New?

swansong of our headlamps dying
sight-read song with the abuelitas in the church basement
song of Madeline and the baby falcon
song for the bakerwoman someone should have married
song to prefer a large stone in our pack to a pebble in a boot
song to our boots and their smell and their easy symbolism
song in the Pink City, in the Old City, in the Wet City

[AN ARRIVAL]

Dominique only knew the word *chicken*. I knew as much
French. He taught me *pression*, as in, draft beer. At the end
of our walking days I dutifully inquired, *pression?* And he
replied, *euh . . . ouais, ouais,* as though deliberating. Look at
us talking! We sat with our beers in mute and marvelous
friendship those first many evenings. He said goodbye a
month ago in Toulouse, kissed my forehead, shouted *ultreïa!*
Today a month later we nearly collide as he walks out of a
bakery in Spain. *San Jacques!* he shouts, arms full of bread,
eyes full of tears. We drink Navarra wine at the shelter,
waving hands and bumbling, without frustration, saying
everything. Zac describes it as speaking in tongues. We
have almost nothing to do with our being here. Marcel is
here, too! Neither man going on to Santiago. They've taken
the way as far as they're able. It has taken twenty years
and twenty pounds off both their aging bodies———

AT HOME IN BEAUTY,
IN BEAUTY AT HOME

In the Pyrenees you find pictures of the Pyrenees.
In wine country, paintings of vineyards.
In a garbage can at the cemetery, a thousand plastic roses.

VINCENT WRITES TO THEO UP TO
NOW I'VE SPENT MORE ON MY COLORS,
CANVASES, ETC. THAN ON MYSELF.
I HAVE ANOTHER NEW ORCHARD FOR
YOU—BUT FOR CHRIST'S SAKE GET THE
PAINT TO ME WITHOUT DELAY

10   Silver white *large* tubes
6   Veronese Green double tubes
3   Lemon chrome yellow
3   No 2   "   "   } double tubes
1   No 3   "   "
1   Vermilion, double tube
3   Geranium lake, small tubes
6   Ordinary lake   "   "   freshly ground,
2   Prussian blue   "   "   if they're greasy
                                     } I'll send them back.
4   Emerald green   "   "

THE COLORS AT
THE BORDERLANDS

After weeks of waking to empty beds
and French silence,
Alister the Norwegian opera star is singing
full-voiced vibrato among the bunkbeds
at 7:30 in the morning
as a team of tanned Spanish cyclists
zip into their suits.
What tool do I pick up now?
That I will not use to scrape...

BEST PRACTICES

Rosary, jack-knife
kept in the same pocket? Smart—
Reach for one, touch both

DEVIL AND GOD POEM

"It is possible you are a saint
 and don't know it," the Devil says to me.

"Well, actually, that's true," God says,
"But only when I say it.
 And you'll notice I didn't say it.
 At least not to you."

"I could kiss you on the mouth for that," I say.

"Me?" they reply in unison.

"Yeah."

song of endless gratitude for Gerard and Tony
song with Sandra and Chantal and the alphorn
songs with Jean-Louis and Benoit,
Robert, Jaki and Genou, Pepe and Juan
song for Marie and Ugit, Dirk, Sven and Diego, Olafia and Jaoiao
Kristian and Ula and Tanya, Nacho, Moe and the taxi
Thomas with the bagpipes
Augustina and her goat risotto
the Salve Regina in the stairwell with Bernard

67

[AN ARRIVAL]

In Grañon a quarter of lamb over potatoes. Tomatoes
from the pharmacist's husband. Then foie gras. My expert
opinion: it's harder to receive than to give. To receive
makes apparent this poor posture. It exposes my place of
origin, requiring a response in a language I don't speak.
Meanwhile giving lets me be a little god and feel good
(evidence I have never truly given either). Surrounded by
candlelight and bedbugs, a Korean man sings a hymn in
his own language. Afterwards says with a heavy accent
through tears, "I can't believe the Son of God came to
this land." For days and weeks after this Zac kept finding
ways to add *to this land* to the end of his sentences——

IN BURGOS

I am a confirmed non-fan
of polychrome statues.
Those caked-on countenances
energized by no life,
not even imagined life.

Give me the worn face
of the wooden Virgin,
with her once-painted eyes
licked closed by time,
finally full of her heart
softened by pain. She undoes
the indignity of duration
with this growth. No self-improvement–
just the direction being would move.

She looks at me, tougher
and more tender than I ever imagined.
Says that *last* means *youngest.*
That I shouldn't trust what doesn't weather well,
That wear is a bloom things do
to set their fruit in time.
She promises me the nothingness
will creep back into things
but it will not
have the youngest word.

MESETA

And the thousand yard shadows

stretch out ahead of you
because the sun

rises
over the Tempranillo vineyards
behind you

CARRION DE LOS CONDES

I led them with human cords, with ropes of love.
—Hosea 11:4

One hard day in Spain
I saw a horse with its bit tethered
To the back of a pickup truck
The farmer slowly drives uphill
A way to get things done
Trudge or dance
The horse named Boanerges

That evening the priest said
Only you and God know why you walk
And probably not even you
He blessed the forehead
Of everyone who walked up
While one sister played the flute
One gave us cut-out paper stars
Saying heaven is no goodbyes

Afterward everyone stumbling around the church
Crying like they were drunk
Terrified of themselves
For having resembled love
For an instant and known it
They weren't ready
They were only people

song to earplugs that might crawl away
song to audition with the Brazilian Synchronized Snoring Team
song still getting up before dawn
song in single file with fields in between
song side by side with a sandwich in between
school children accompaniment along the playground fence
beat of red grasshoppers thumping off sleeves
song fighting dogs with a hiking pole
song for the death of the automobile

[AN ARRIVAL]

The sign outside the church of Virgen del Encina read: *Nadie pase por aqui sin saludar a Maria y decirle con amor no me dejes madre mia.* Let no one pass by without greeting Mary and saying with love don't leave me my mother. Two hours of songs that night thanks to a pilgrim with a guitarlele and lyrics in a dozen languages. Pointing at someone, "where are you from?" then singing to them in their tongue. We joined in recklessly. Late October. The endingness affecting us like strong wine, loving one another as if we'd been close all our lives. My favorite song was the one that consisted almost entirely of jumping up and down, arms around the person next to you, shouting *weh weh weh weh wehhhhh, weh weh weh weh wehhhhhhh* into their face. I think it was in Czech———

FERROUS FOLK REMEDY

Go and take this page and write on it
the name of every person you can think of
who has cheated, harmed, embarrassed,
shamed, humiliated, degraded,
ignored, bothered, wounded,
offended, tricked, betrayed
or wronged you in any way.
Don't forget to write your own.

Find a palm-sized stone and wrap it in this paper.
Draw a simple face on it.
It's your face the day you were born.
Hold it in your hands and say:
I am sorry I left you to bear this weather alone
thank you for lighting this tenderness fire
I love—I want to love—why you came to this land

Lay it down among the others in the pile.
Open your empty hands and eyes.
Who is the one smiling? Why now?
Better say hello.

STRANGER

We dodge olives by day
and also eat them

Though she is too old
a blonde Spaniard drinks chocolate milk

I too refute the existence of time

Overwhelmed by a sense that long ago
there is someone asking
me to pray for them

    A broken castle in a field

    Another

TERRACOTTA

I will forget most of my life
making any narrative
porous fabrication—
Homo faber as in
Which holm oak?
Who biked to bring the orange juice?
Did I peek in a stone granary?

Better the asp eat the lizard
and leave oblivion out of it.
A star in the belly, or heartbeat in a wound.
A gorge on grace, then basically motionless
for years, call it building.

THE WORD REMEMBER IS BROKEN

Years later I find something I wrote here but can't remember
why:

A singleness came over, I saw the beauty and welled, I said to God,
I love you and I am sorry if I forget this moment.

song that long-johns are considered formal dinnerwear
song while giving blisters nicknames
lullaby under newspaper at a bus stop
song for the bedbugs who bit Chanti's eyes closed
song for thatched or other very nicely shaped roofs
songs of the past to help the present
songs of the present to help the future
song of David already returning from where you are going

[AN ARRIVAL]

"Sorry, all full," he said in Spanish after hanging up the
fake phone call, "that was tour bus of Christians, and they
have a priest, so they have priority." Then vanished into
the kitchen, visibly rattled from such gratuitous lying.
Must have been a kind man. When he returned a woman
entered. It was obvious that he hadn't the heart to either
lie to her or come clean to us. Instead he lost control. "You
camino tourists, how shameful to take advantage of us
and our house of God, you don't know what it is to be a
pilgrim, back when I was a pilgrim —..." When I recall
that day I see the wind blowing the dying grasses around
the mountainside and the town sailing like a flotilla on
a choppy gold sea. A perfect day. I remember this vividly.
Not my heart drumming my furious response, not putting
"house of God" in quotes for him, not the man's eyes
straight down, the woman dumbfounded, my friend turned
sideways. Not all of us carved solid in silence, figureheads
on prows of ships facing directions we weren't going ———

NOW AND NOT YET

Step into the light, poor Lazarus
— Gillian Welch

A day can break your heart in a day
All over you as if you weren't even there
It's a different knowing, going is
Intimacy of discovery drowning
Kissing toward origins as they zoom by
You wake in one place
If you wish to end somewhere else
Your body must be what takes you there

Zac stayed behind at one point
His desert days so called
After which his body showed up at the door at noon
Wrecked eyes in a face
He wasn't the same
Walked alone most of the time
Spirit (w)ringing his dreaming
While there's still time

Now to walk with him today
Was like I haven't seen him in years
Singing, talking, praying
Sounds coming back from his soundings
Someone right here became his face
After yesterday what are you supposed to be
We could say to any day

O

A break in the tree line

last week's lands appear impossible

must it require the same faith
to believe backward
as to believe —in any direction, or none— Ostriches
in a eucalyptus forest

song for the worst days ending in oblivion
song for the best days ending in oblivion
fiddle tune that ends if and when we say
song to protest irrealities proposed by loneliness
song that speaks for emptiness
song of the horses of O Cebreiro
song while sketching a picture of a spire

[EXCERPT FROM FIRST SERMON OF VINCENT VAN GOGH, OCTOBER 26, 1876]

I once saw a very beautiful picture: it was a landscape at evening. In the distance on the right-hand side a row of hills appeared blue in the evening mist. Above those hills the splendor of the sunset, the grey clouds with their linings of silver and gold and purple. The landscape is a plain or heath covered with grass and its yellow leaves, for it was in autumn. Through the landscape a road leads to a high mountain far, far away, on the top of that mountain is a city wherein the setting sun casts a glory. On the road walks a pilgrim, staff in hand. He has been walking for a good long while already and he is very tired. And now he meets a woman, or figure in black, that makes one think of St. Paul's word: As being sorrowful yet always rejoicing. That Angel of God has been placed there to encourage the pilgrims and to answer their questions and the pilgrim asks her: Does the road go uphill, then, all the way? And the answer is: Yes to the very end———

TWO OR THREE A PARADE /
THE NARROW WAY

The heart never fits the journey.
Always one ends first.
And then there's all these people
kissing eyelids in a meadow
brought through the gate
one after another.

HALLOWEEN

It is raining on Lavacolla.

After enough rain one unburdens oneself of attempts to stay dry.

And after enough rain one may endeavor, quit of one's garments,
to send the body alone

to find how wet the rain.

↶

Faces are thin places and too much to handle at the moment.
I've always felt a face should be the one place where the ghosts
    aren't.

↶

Tonight we recognize the power of masks.

The I is the best mask.

And I've worn the costume of an eager shepherd;
the precious cargo, hoofs and everything, slung over his shoulders
until he forgot it was there.

Only the light warmth around his neck initiates him
into the mystery of becoming-what-you've-done.

↶

The chosen love so unapparent in the doing.

↶

Too heavy only when I try to set it down.

song of what only you know about God
song to never save for special occasions
song to answer: who told you you were naked?
song in a vineyard about a vineyard
song of the thorny crowned kinglet
that song again forgive me

[AN ARRIVAL]

Wasn't holiness burned my heart. Investigated chest
pocket: phone burned my hand, flashing white hot
death throes across its face. Looked up immediately
to St. James behind the altar: expressionless. Zac next
to me in the pew: unaware. The botafumiero censer
starts to swing smoke over a colorful sea of rain jackets.
Everything — photo, video, note, address, field recording —
every last thing rises up, mingles with incense near the
Cathedral ceiling, and is gone. Offered up I see. *For all the
saints* (we'd been singing it for days). For all the saints
who hum for us now through the thin wall the songs
they wove from living. It's enough, living. The opening
procession stops for a moment next to our pew. Next
verse they keep walking. We, as it happens, do not——

FIELD OF STARS

Stones bloom above, soggy green banners
of this backyard wedding
welcome last guests,
oxygen blows however deep underground
fanning our torches brightly
in the body-night. So wind, so time.
Gifts toward which, tilting, we marry
ourselves as an instrument
to the remaining melody. By cleaving
such forces do we ever send our crumpled paper ships
home. I dreamt all night about home.
I was in my heart. Who am I who is ready
to go there.

FURTHERANCE

First your face.
The sun blesses it
off. Then night chars
your belly with the scent
of mountain mint.

At the next crossing
you look ahead
and say
this will make me too different
from the ones I love.

Then you are a new moon,
bright on the away side,
in the ascendant
with none to see.

Authenticated in the wild,
you speak good distance now.
You have tethered
your tribe to other lands,
and not out loud.

See.
You are a half-moon.
A sideways tunnel.
Light on both ends.

SATURDAY

The sunburst across the mouth of a cave,
the way it rings what maybe is.

Or the nonlight inside,
depending on where we are.

A thing is beautiful if we see its nothingness
losing to love.

If it resembles a yes
we would resemble sometimes.

If it ends giddier than it begins
complicating the person we remain.

Meanwhile. We are the Saturday people
staring at our hands in the dark,

calibrating our whole lives by that looking.
Sitting in here with the dead

Christ imagining that if it is him
he'll make the first move.

We get tired waiting. We nod. We fall
asleep. Dream we are walking along a windbreak
    of holly.

One hand in his and one running
along the shiny spiked leaves almost

painlessly. We wake alone
the color of stone burnished by morning.

NOTES

On a dark night / The author's translation and reworking of the first stanza of the St. John of the Cross poem "Una Noche Oscura" into the form of a fiddle tune. It is meant for improvisational fiddle accompaniment.

songs without plan / An early working title for this collection, and what Thomas Merton called the Psalms, for "there is no blueprint for ecstasy."

KIND OF LIGHT / The first line comes from Psalm 139.

DISTANCE LOVES BLUE / These are words of John O'Donohue from his book *Beauty: The Invisible Embrace* (2004).

TWO SONGS FOR CARDABELLE / *Cardabelle* is the local name for a mountain thistle they hang on doors in Southern France; it prophesies rain and wards off evil. See drawing on page 86.

THE LAST WORDS THE MAGPIE HEARD... / This poem is a retelling of a folktale from the town of St. Guilhem le Desert.

TORCHLIGHT PROCESSION / "Hell of mercy, not of wrath" is a quote from Bl. Isaac of Stella. This poem is dedicated to the pilgrims at Lourdes in search of healing.

Love made a sphere / "Love made a sphere" is a line from Robert Lax's *Circus of the Sun*. Many aspects of this book are indebted to Lax. This poem is also meant for fiddle accompaniment.

WE TRY WRITING A PILGRIM PRAYER / Co-written with Zac Chastain.

VINCENT WRITES TO THEO... / Assembled from a letter to Theo van Gogh from Arles, on or about Thursday, 5 April

1888. Van Gogh Letters Project in Association with the Van Gogh Museum and the Huygens Institute.

[EXCERPT FROM FIRST SERMON...] / Delivered by Van Gogh at the Wesleyan Methodist Church in Richmond, England on Sunday, 29 October 1876. Van Gogh Letters Project in Association with the Van Gogh Museum and the Huygens Institute.

TWO OR THREE A PARADE / The first two lines are drawn from the Jack Gilbert poem "Islands and Figs."

HALLOWEEN / Dedicated to Franz Wright. The words "the I is the best mask" are his.

A note on the drawings / They are what remained in the author's sketchbook at the end of the journey, with regrets that he could not offer more, as the rest—and the best—were given away, left as thank-yous at shelters, or traded for things.

GRATITUDES

Thank you to the editors at *Cleveland Review of Books*, *TriQuarterly*, *Northern New England Review*, *Peripheries*, *On the Seawall*, *Presence*, and *Windfall Room* where versions of these poems first appeared. Thanks as well to composer Christian Martin who set an earlier version of "Two Songs for Cardabelle" to original music and performed it with the Princeton Singers. Sweet thanks to Sarah Frank and Luke Fraser of The Bombadils, who took this poet on the road where we performed many of these poems live on stage, often with music, including an early "crankie" version of "The Last Words the Magpie Heard . . . "

The primary and most insufficient thanks are to my family. My parents, Tony and Patti, my brothers Tony and Vince, Katie and the kids, grandparents, cousins, aunts and uncles. And to the family of friends I've been given and blessed with, too many to name. Thank you, all of you, for your presence and love in my life. This book is for you.

My gratefulness and admiration goes out to my teachers Dara Barrois/Dixon, Peter Gizzi, James Tate, and Lynn Xu. For their insights, poetic companionship, and/or help with this work along its journey, I thank David Feinstein, John Sieracki, Alex Andreosatos, Isaac Slater, Tim Taranto, John Knight, Rebecca Dinerstein-Knight, Courtney Hartman, Urban Hannon, Ron Slate, Joe Rosta, Hannah Maverick Cruz, Alexis Almeida, Alex Morris, Logan Hill, Lindsey Webb, Adam Marston, John Goodhue, Emma De Lisle, Zach Savich, Sally Read. An especially deep thanks to Dara and Emma for their generosity with this manuscript at various stages.

Thanks as well to the many communities who have offered heavenly and earthly support in the making of this book: Con-solatio, Mt. Saviour Monastery, Vermont Studio Center,

Woolman Hill, St. Marys Monastery & St. Scholastica Priory, Forbes Library, Catena Artistorum, and Nine Athens Music. Special thanks to the Powel family for time at Brook's Cabin. To Rob, Lynette, Katherine and John, thank you. Thank you to Kari and John Riess and all at Angelico Press for the work and vision to bring this book to life, and to Lauren Peters-Collaer for deigning to turn a humble sketch into a wildly beautiful cover.

To my pilgrim family I encountered/accumulated along the way, many who are named in this book, thank you. You are the blessing that lives on in me. To all the communities along the Camino, all the shelters and parishes, all the hospitaleros and volunteers, thank you. To all who gave me your prayer intentions to carry, it was in bringing them to Santiago that I was brought along as well. This book is as much for you all as it is for anyone.

Besides Vincent Van Gogh and those whose names appear in this work, I want to acknowledge the many celestial pilgrims who have made their presence known and to whom I owe an enormous debt of gratitude: Emily Dickinson, Federico Garcia Lorca, Gerard Manley Hopkins, Roger Scruton, Simone Weil, Joseph Ceravolo, Basho, Ezra Pound, Hans Urs von Balthasar, Bl. Jacopone da Todi, St. John Henry Newman, King David, Isaiah, Julian of Norwich, St. Catherine of Siena, St. Roch, St. Pio of Pietrelcina, St. Paul, St. Augustine, St. Thomas Aquinas, St. Francis of Assisi, St. Clare, St. Nicholas.

The poet Elizabeth Barrett Browning apparently asked Charles Kingsley, "What's the secret of your life? Tell me, that I may make mine beautiful also." And he replied, "I had a friend." How many people along the Camino asked us, Zac, the secret of our friendship, when it itself is the secret, eternally right on time. From one wannabe holy fool to another, thank you.

A final thanks to you, reader, for travelling so far with me. Both then and now. May you hear the call of St. James and go. As for me, I have tried to offer this book with back to the world with the same generosity it was given, with joy but also with no small amount of trepidation, since *peregrinatio est tacere,* as the Desert Fathers wrote. One translation: "to be a pilgrim is to keep silent." And the sharper Abba Tithoes version: "pilgrimage means a man should control his tongue." Pray for mercy on this pilgrim, who, without a doubt, did not sufficiently control his pen.

> Glory to God
> for all things.

www.ingramcontent.com/pod-product-compliance
Lightning Source LLC
Chambersburg PA
CBHW022033090426
42741CB00007B/1052